THIS POEM DOESN'T RHYME

'What a delight to read a collection that doesn't assume that children can only cope with agreeable twaddle ... And what a pleasure it is to see an anthologist encouraging new readers to recognize the way that the metrical "music" of good poetry leaves its imprint on the mind.' – Peter Holding, Signal Poetry Award judge.

In this hugely entertaining anthology Gerard Benson seeks to dispel the fixed idea held by so many children that poetry has to rhyme. He opens up a whole new range of experience through alliteration, assonance, eye–rhyme, repetition, neologism, haiku, riddles and shape poems, and also releases their imaginations to write their own poetry, unconstrained by regularly chiming line ends.

A wonderful introduction to the infinite possibilities of poetry.

Gerard Benson is a poet, story-teller and performer who, although now based in Bradford, runs workshops and courses all around the country with children and adults. A former lecturer for twenty years at the Central School of Speech and Drama, and a professionally trained actor, he is a member of the Barrow Poets, a group which performed poetry and music all over Britain, Germany, Holland and North America in its hey-day, but which has become 'fairly inactive' now. Still active are the story-telling concerts he does with pianist Jean Phillips – known as the Gerard and Jean Concerts.

THIS POEM DOESN'T RHYME

Edited by Gerard Benson

Illustrated by Sarah-Jane Stewart

PUFFIN BOOKS

To Cathy with love

PUFFIN BOOKS

Published by the Penguin Group
Penguin Books Ltd, 27 Wrights Lane, London W8 5TZ, England
Penguin Books USA Inc., 375 Hudson Street, New York, New York 10014, USA
Penguin Books Australia Ltd, Ringwood, Victoria, Australia
Penguin Books Canada Ltd, 10 Alcorn Avenue, Toronto, Ontario, Canada M4V 3B2
Penguin Books (NZ) Ltd, 182–190 Wairau Road, Auckland 10, New Zealand

Penguin Books Ltd, Registered Offices: Harmondsworth, Middlesex, England

This collection first published by Viking 1990
Published in Puffin Books 1992
1 3 5 7 9 10 8 6 4 2

This collection copyright © Gerard Benson, 1990
Illustrations copyright © Sarah-Jane Stewart, 1990
All rights reserved

Copyright information for individual poems is given on pages 159–160
which constitute an extension of this copyright page

The moral right of the author has been asserted

Printed in England by Clays Ltd, St Ives plc

CONTENTS

ANIMALS OUT OF THE CAGE

OBJECTS MADE FROM WORDS

HEAR MY VOICE

POEMS TO SEE AND HEAR

CHARACTER STUDIES

INTERVIEW WITH THE EDITOR

What are you doing on this page? This isn't your part of the book.

We'd like to ask you a few questions about the poems you've chosen.

Go ahead.

Well, first: Don't you like rhyme?

I love it – sometimes.

Then why have you made a book of poems that don't rhyme?

When I've talked to children, I've found that lots of them think that poetry *must* rhyme, above all else. It often spoils what they write.

How?

For instance, one girl wrote a very promising beginning to a poem about a horse – but once she'd mentioned the stable, she added a table and even a girl called Mabel.

What's wrong with that? It sounds quite funny.

She wasn't trying to write a funny poem. She wanted to express what she felt about an animal that had excited her imagination. The rhyme distracted her. I thought a book of unrhymed poetry might help readers to see other possibilities.

If it doesn't rhyme, how do you know it's a poem?

That's a hard question. And I haven't got a foolproof answer. A poem is an object made from words. It might do one of many things. It could be a description, an expression of deep feeling, a joke, a discussion, a prayer or a simple story. Whatever kind of poem it is, the language usually has a pattern of some kind. Rhyme is one way of patterning words.

What other ways are there?

Plenty. Repetition is important. In 'Hiawatha', the rhythm is very strong and repetitive and the poet repeats particular words. In the old poetry of England the beginning letters of words are repeated.

I've heard of that, it's called alliteration. But rhyming poets use that too.

That's true. So do the people who write newspaper headlines. Another element in poetry — far more important than rhyme — is metaphor.

What's that?

What I call 'magical transformations'. If you call a lake a mirror, or the sun a fried egg, that is a metaphor.

Are there any metaphors in this book?

Lots. Have a look through. There's a poem by Emily Dickinson that seems to be about a horse but if you read it carefully . . .

The dustbin-liner poem is full of metaphors.

It is. And it's rather like a riddle.

There are lots of riddles, aren't there?

Yes. I like riddles. They play about with words and ideas in a creative way.

Where did you find all the poems?

I read some in books and magazines. Some the poets sent me. One or two were written specially, and I even found one framed on a bedroom wall.

Which one?

Guess.

Why did you choose those particular ones?

I thought children would like to read them. That's the main thing. And they show different approaches to writing that I thought some readers would like to try.

Was it difficult to choose them?

Very. I had to leave out many fine poems.

Are all the poems by English writers?

Quite a lot are, but there are poems by American, West Indian, African, Indian, Chinese, Irish, Scots, Welsh writers and others.

Are any of the poems by children?

One was written by a twelve-year-old Victorian boy. I so admired his skill and his verve and his sense of humour, I felt I had to include him.

Have you any message for children who read this book?

Enjoy it. Write some poems of your own.

Will you put in an introduction saying all this, so that children can understand why you made the book?

No. People don't usually read introductions. And anyway, it's more interesting talking to you.

*It doesn't have to rhyme
there are other ways*

Problems of Poetry

There was a young poet of Tring
Whose poetry never would rhyme,
    When I asked him the reason,
    He sighed, 'It's the Time of Year.
I never can rhyme round about Christmas.'

        (Oh dear!)
            (Try again!)
        (Here goes!)

There was a young bard from the Isthmus
Whose poetry was rhythmless (that's better!)
    When I asked him the reason
    He groaned, 'It's the Time of Year.
I can't get it right in the Spr . . .
(Oh dash. It's autumn!)'

So he sat at his desk and he cried
And his chest it did heave like the sea going
                                    in and out,
    'Oh I can't get it together
    Whether it's sunny or raining.'
So he went to his bed, but he didn't even die.

Gerard Benson

Another method

I am a prose poem
this is my second line
and this my third
I consist of fifteen lines in all
these made up from a total
of seventy one words.
I am neither beautiful
nor am I ugly
and I differ from all other poems
in that I describe nothing
except myself.
Where, when and by whom I was written
is therefore unimportant.
I have no title, and finish
abruptly.

Nick Toczek

Well, it looks *like a rhyming one!*

Jack and Jill

Jack told his sister, Jill, that they should climb
The mighty hill, at risk of life and limb
And, once they'd reached the well upon the height,
They'd fill their pail and then would share
                                 the weight.
He'd find the pail too heavy on his own,
But sharing they could quickly bring it down.
So off they started, Jack was in the lead
Until he tripped and fell upon his head.
Dame Margery was out and keeping watch
With vinegar and paper bags to patch
Jack's head and, when she heard Jill's mocking
                                 laughter,
She was extremely angry with her daughter.
You'd be surprised to hear the things she said
And all the horrid names she called the maid.
Besides she whacked her smartly on her rear,
Jill bellowed, this was more than she could bear.

John Sweetman

Haiku

Poem in three lines:
Five syllables, then seven,
Five again; no rhyme.

Eric Finney

Highcoo

Up on the ledges
Above the city traffic:
Fond sounds of pigeons.

Eric Finney

Hicuckoo!

Back again so soon?
Or is it just those mad boys
Fooling in the wood?

Eric Finney

Cinquain

Cinquain:
A short verse form
Of counted syllables . . .
And first devised by Adelaide
Crapsey.

Gerard Benson

The Warning

Just now,
Out of the strange
Still dusk . . as strange, as still . .
A white moth flew. Why am I grown
So cold?

Adelaide Crapsey

Blank verse – ten syllables stride in five steps

from The Passing of Arthur

The other swiftly strode from ridge to ridge,
Clothed with his breath, and looking, as he walked,
Larger than human on the frozen hills.
He heard the deep behind him, and a cry
Before. His own thought drove him like a goad.
Dry clashed his harness in the icy caves
And barren chasms, and all to left and right
The bare black cliff clanged round him, as he based
His feet on juts of slippery crags that rang
Sharp-smitten with the dint of armèd heels –
And on a sudden, lo! the level lake,
And the long glories of the winter moon.

Alfred Lord Tennyson

When you read John Mole's fine poem 'The Shoes' on page 119, you may hear this rhythm echoed

from The Song of Hiawatha

Blessing the Cornfields

Sing, O Song of Hiawatha,
Of the happy days that followed,
In the land of the Ojibways,
In the pleasant land and peaceful!
Sing the mysteries of Mondamin,
Sing the Blessing of the Cornfields!
   Buried was the bloody hatchet,
Buried was the dreadful war-club,
Buried were all warlike weapons,
And the war-cry was forgotten.
There was peace among the nations;
Unmolested roved the hunters,
Built the birch canoe for sailing,
Caught the fish in lake and river,
Shot the deer and trapped the beaver;
Unmolested worked the women,
Made their sugar from the maple,
Gathered wild rice in the meadows,
Dressed the skins of deer and beaver.
   All around the happy village
Stood the maize-fields, green and shining,
Waved the green plumes of Mondamin,
Waved his soft and sunny tresses,
Filling all the land with plenty.
'T was the women who in Spring-time

Planted the broad fields and fruitful,
Buried in the earth Mondamin;
'T was the women who in Autumn
Stripped the yellow husks of harvest,
Stripped the garments from Mondamin,
Even as Hiawatha taught them.

H. W. Longfellow

Coochi-coochi

By the supermarket trollee,
In an eezi-fold-up buggee,
Underneath a quilto-kumfi
Lay the sacred infant dribbling,
And he spoke the tongue of tinies,
Sang the tongue of Not-Yet-Toddler,
'Oba-gurgle, oogle-oo-goo,
Bubba-dubba, mummee-wah-wah,
Urkle-gobba, plugga-wagga,
Blubbli-obblah!' wailed the infant
Till his mummee, Mrs Buncer,
Plugged his cakehole with a dummee,
Dummee dipped in maple syrup,
As approached a gushing grannee.
Grannee exited from Tesco,
From the quik-food in the freezer,
Looked into the fold-up buggee,
Whispered 'Coochi-mudjekeewis,
Husa-booti fula-babba,
Izzaneetha spitta-dadda,'
Called him 'Coochi-mudjekeewis,'
Even though his name was Jason
(Full name Jason Kristin Buncer),
He who plucked away his dummee,
Blew the sacred wind upon her,
Sicked upon the avocado
In the Tesco bag of grannee.

Bill Greenwell

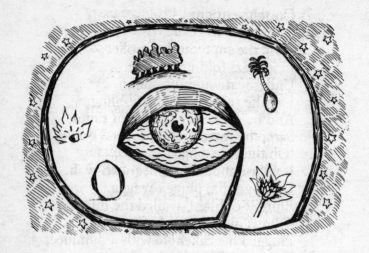

Spell of Creation

Within the flower there lies a seed,
Within the seed there springs a tree,
Within the tree there spreads a wood.

In the wood there burns a fire,
And in the fire there melts a stone,
Within the stone a ring of iron.

Within the ring there lies an O
Within the O there looks an eye,
In the eye there swims a sea,

And in the sea reflected sky,
And in the sky there shines the sun,
Within the sun a bird of gold.

Within the bird there beats a heart,
And from the heart there flows a song,
And in the song there sings a word.

In the word there speaks a world,
A word of joy, a world of grief,
From joy and grief there springs my love.

Oh love, my love, there springs a world,
And on the world there shines a sun
And in the sun there burns a fire,

Within the fire consumes my heart
And in my heart there beats a bird,
And in the bird there wakes an eye,

Within the eye, earth, sea and sky,
Earth, sky and sea within an O
Lie like the seed within the flower.

Kathleen Raine

Full Moon
I

A cannon ball,
A lost balloon,
A peppermint,
A pool of lead.

A mighty lump
Of porridge limp,
A lamp, a polished
Dustbin lid.

The hubcap from
An autoroute,
The helmet of
An astronaut.

A mottled dish,
Or disc at dusk,
Will sink almost,
(It mostly must,)
In mist, or moistly
Float.

Discuss.

*William
Bealby-Wright*

*If we don't want to rhyme we can repeat the word
instead*

A Nail

For want of a nail, the shoe was lost;
For want of a shoe, the horse was lost;
For want of a horse, the rider was lost;
For want of a rider, the battle was lost;
For want of a battle, the kingdom was lost:
And all for want of a horseshoe nail.

Anon.

Seven Activities for a Young Child

Turn on the tap for straight and silver
                  water in the sink,
Cross your finger through
The sleek thread falling   — *One*

Spread white sandgrains on a tray,
And make clean furrows with a bent stick
To stare for a meaning   — *Two*

Draw some clumsy birds on yellow paper,
Confronting each other and as if to fly
Over your scribbled hill   — *Three*

Cut rapid holes into folded paper, look
At the unfolded pattern, look
Through the unfolded pattern   — *Four*

Walk on any square stone of the pavement,
Or on any crack between, as long
As it's with no one or with someone   — *Five*

Throw up a ball to touch the truest brick
Of the red brick wall,
Catch it with neat, cupped hand   — *Six*

Make up in your head a path, and name it,
Name where it will lead you,
Walk towards where it will lead you   — *Seven*

One, two, three, four, five, six, seven:
Take up the-rag-doll-quietly-and-sing-her- to-sleep.

Alan Brownjohn

Working in Winter

Silently the snow settles on the scaffolding,
The feathery flakes flurry and flick their fragments,
The brown bricks piled on billowing polythene
Heap their heaviness to heavenly heights.
Workmen in woolly hats whistle into the wind
Or dance in donkey jackets to hold in heat,
Their toes tingle, the tips of their fingers freeze –
It's murder, mate, this job is, murder.
Roll on five o'clock!

John Mole

29

Try naming *the letters instead of reading them.*
You'll need to read it several times!

```
            a b . . . y z . . . i c . . . q e d

        r           u           i           c
        o           i           c
        o           i           c       u       r
        r           u           a
        r           u           b
        i           c
        r           u
        y           r           u
        o           y           r       u
        r           u           y
        r           u           z
        i           c
        u           r
        i           c           u       r
        i           c
```

Bob Cobbing

A picture in words . . . not only ordinary letters are used but the morse code as well. This is also an acrostic – or perhaps an 'upstick'!

Forsythia

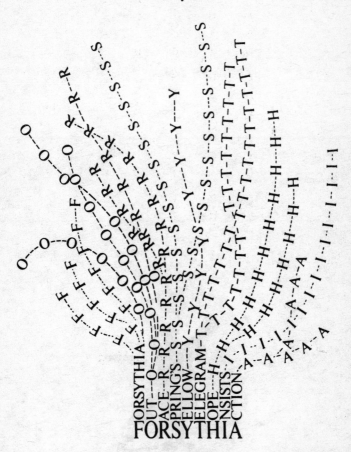

Mary Ellen Solt

Rhythms of the landscape

Spray

It is a wonder foam is so beautiful.
A wave bursts in anger on a rock, broken up
in wild white sibilant spray
and falls back, drawing in its breath with rage,
with frustration how beautiful!

D. H. Lawrence

Sea-Weed

Sea-weed sways and sways and swirls
as if swaying were its form of stillness;
and if it flushes against fierce rock
it slips over it as shadows do, without hurting itself.

D. H. Lawrence

Freedom

I am going where the green grass grows
And fields flaunt their wild flowers;
Where swallows swoop and skim under the sallows
And the clear river shimmers
In summer sunshine.

Behind me lies the dust of dreary city
And the toiling troubled traffic;
People pushing past;
Litter lying unlovely in lay-bys.

High on the hills hawks hover
And larks rise singing sonatas to the sunrise.
Where the grass blows in the wind
I shall lie and listen to the birdsong and
Silence.

Mary Dawson

from The Vision of Piers Plowman

'After sharp showers,' said Peace, 'how shining
the sun!
There's no weather warmer, than after watery
clouds.
Nor any love that has more delight, nor friendship
fonder,
Than after war and woe, when Love and Peace are
the masters.
Never was war in this world, nor wickedness so
cruel,
But that Love, if he liked, could bring all to laughing,
And Peace, through patience, put stop to all perils.'

William Langland

A Dirty Night on the Fastnet Rock

Oh Flutes! the night came on,
   The grizzly, guzzling, gulping night,
And oh Great Scott what mud, what rain,
                             what scrunch!
   The rain came down in streams –
   'Twas not the spitting, cat-like rain, oh no! –
It was the swilling, swelching, Swithian rain
   That makes the new rags and the old alike
                             smell wet,
     The sousing, duck-loved rain.

The wind grew worse; oh slithering snow-shoes how
                            it squelched!
   It screeched around the lighthouse like some
                       green-eyed fiend –
   Great Scotland Yard what shrieks!
The one-stringed fiddle or the untuned flute were
                   music to those shrieks;

The swinging, swelching, slobbering waves came
                   lamming on the rocks,
   The gulching, sea-green waves.
And as I looked, I saw an awful distant sky-high
                        wave,
   Land's End it was a wave!
Afar it seemed an oily, bloated, bulging wave,
                       but near
   It was a swearing, oathing, spiteful wave!
                     buzzing along,
   A Boss-Eyed Shaker, yet a beastly wave.

Great Scott! it nears the rock,
   The many-cornered, wave-dividing rock.
It humped itself upon its strong hind legs and
                        then it burst
   It more than burst, it bust, it simply bashed,
It lit upon the blistered rock and swept away the
                        lighthouse lamp,
   The beastly oily lighthouse lamp.

Oh Hares! Oh Jumping Crimes!
   Oh shattering chandeliers and fizzing squish!
   Oh creeping crocodiles and crippled crabs!
It gulched and slooched around the scraggy
                        lighthouse rock,
   The well-pecked lobster rock.

Oh Flutes! the night came on –
   The grizzly, grimy, black-eyed night, a night that
                        gloried in being black.
My tooth-gnawed pen can ill describe the inky
                        darkness of that congealed black.
Suffice to say the Patagonian slug
   Would shine like muzzled virtue next that black.

But hold! what is that shadowy form?
   Oh scootling wizards! Can I see aright?
A ship! An uncouth, ghastly, scarecrow ship!
   With fear I shrink away, and like the unspun
                        spinning top
   I hold my breath.

Oh Snakes! she nears the rock,
    The many-cornered, wave-dividing rock –
Oh splathering toads! I see the masts and gear,
    The spinning wheel, the death's head on the prow.
I see the horror-stricken victims clinging to the ropes,
    A ghastly lot, unshaven, a filthy, dirty, beastly-
                                        looking crew,
Huddled upon an unscrubbed, an unswabbed and
                                unsqueegeed deck –
    Oh one-eyed Crusoe let me die unknown,
    A gasping cod-fish on some puffin's isle,
But let me never gaze again on such a sight!

On came the humping bulging waves
    Bearing their wobbling craft,
The hog-backed, quivering, floundering craft.
Oh staggering jelly how she reels,
Oh shivering custard and oh writhing eels,
Oh bandaged thunder and oh lightning greased,
    Oh palsied, lurching, epileptic funk,
    With one last agonising buck-jump leap
She's whizzed a splathered wreck upon the rock
        And sunk!

Rev. William Packenham-Walsh (written at the age of twelve)

41

Child on Top of a Greenhouse

The wind billowing out the seat of my britches,
My feet crackling splinters of glass and dried putty,
The half-grown chrysanthemums staring up like
accusers,
Up through the streaked glass, flashing with sunlight,
A few white clouds all rushing eastward,
A line of elms plunging and tossing like horses,
And everyone, everyone pointing up and shouting!

Theodore Roethke

Wind

Wind would tear a dead man's shroud,
Wind as sharp as edge of spade,
Wind as keen as tip of axe,
Wind that swoops like bearded shot,
Wind umbrella-like in form,
Wind that fills the sea with bones,
Wind that levels all before it.

Malay . . . Anon.

Snow and Ice

As birds flying he scattereth the snow,
And the falling down thereof
Is as the lighting of grasshoppers:
The eye marvelleth at the beauty
Of the whiteness thereof, and the heart
Is astonished at the raining of it.

The hoarfrost also as salt he poureth on the earth,
And being congealed, it lieth on top of sharp stakes.

When the cold north wind bloweth,
And the water is congealed into ice,
It abideth upon every gathering together of water,
And clotheth the water
As with a breastplate.

Son of Sirach
(Book of Ecclesiasticus)

Woodcut

A horseman riding
the wide plains of Eltrim
sees three leagues before him
a great demesne-wall
and windows of a house
the woods have laid siege to.

I watch him from a distance
give the head to his hunter
and take at a gallop
a gap in the stonework
till red coat and chestnut
are lost in the coppice.

Three things October
has shown me this evening,
the first shorn ash-tree
the last swallow gone
and a rider and horse
the woods have laid siege to.

R. N. D. Wilson

Slieve Gua

Slieve Gua, craggy and black wolf-den:
    In its clefts the wind howls,
    In its denes the wolves wail.

Autumn on Slieve Gua: and the angry
    Brown deer bells, and herons
    Croak across Slieve Gua's crags.

Trans. from the Old Irish

Pleasant Sounds

The rustling of leaves under the feet in woods and
    under hedges;
The crumping of cat-ice and snow down wood-rides,
    narrow lanes, and every street causeway;
Rustling through a wood or rather rushing, while the
    wind halloos in the oak-top like thunder;
The rustle of birds' wings startled from their nests or
    flying unseen into the bushes;
The whizzing of larger birds overhead in a wood,
    such as crows, puddocks, buzzards;
The trample of robins and woodlarks on the brown
    leaves, and the patter of squirrels on the green
    moss;
The fall of an acorn on the ground, the pattering of
    nuts on the hazel branches as they fall from
    ripeness;
The flirt of the groundlark's wing from the stubbles –
    how sweet such pictures on dewy mornings,
    when the dew flashes from its brown feathers!

John Clare

Their Beauty Has More Meaning

Yesterday morning enormous the moon hung low on
the ocean,
Round and yellow-rose in the glow of dawn;
The night-herons flapping home wore dawn on their
wings. Today
Black is the ocean, black and sulphur the sky,
And white seas leap. I honestly do not know which
day is more beautiful.
I know that tomorrow or next year or in twenty
years
I shall not see these things – and it does not matter,
it does not hurt;
They will be here. And when the whole human race
Has been like me rubbed out, they will still be here:
storms, moon and ocean,
Dawn and the birds. And I say this: their beauty has
more meaning
Than the whole human race and the race of birds.

Robinson Jeffers

47

from **A Boy's Poem**

The village lights were sprinkled on the hill;
And on the dim and solitary loch,
Our oar-blades stirred the sea to phantom light,
A hoary track ran glimmering from the keel.

Like scattered embers of a dying fire,
The village lights had burnt out one by one;
I lay awake and heard at intervals
A drowsy wave break helpless on the shore,
Trailing the rattling pebbles as it washed
Back to the heaving gloom. By sweet degrees
My slumberous being closed its weary leaves
In drowsy bliss, and slowly sank in dream.

Alexander Smith

Night Clouds

The white mares of the moon rush along the sky
Beating their golden hoofs upon the glass Heavens;
The white mares of the moon are all standing on
                                    their hind legs
Pawing at the green porcelain doors of the remote
                                    Heavens.
Fly, mares!
Strain your utmost,
Scatter the milky dust of stars,
Or the tiger sun will leap upon you and destroy you
With one lick of his vermilion tongue.

Amy Lowell

from Evening: by a Tailor

Day hath put on his jacket, and around
His burning bosom buttoned it with stars.
Here will I lay me on the velvet grass,
That is like padding to earth's meagre ribs,
And hold communion with the things about me.
Ah me! how lovely is the golden braid
That binds the skirt of night's descending robe!
The thin leaves, quivering on their silken threads,
Do make a music like to rustling satin,
As the light breezes smooth their downy nap.

Oliver Wendell Holmes

from To Beauty

Bring me knowledge:
How the pansies are made, and the cuckoos' song!
And the little owls, grey in the evening, three
                                        on a gate;
The gold-cups a-field, the flight of the swallow;
The eyes of the cow who has calved;
The wind passing from ash-tree to ash-tree!

John Galsworthy

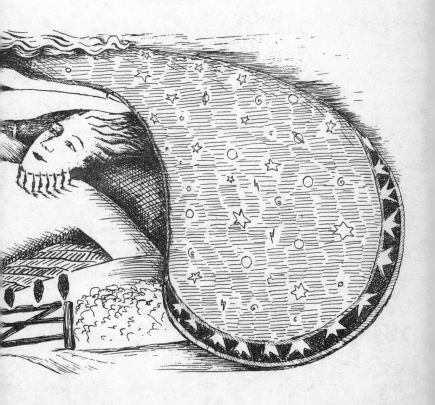

Water Picture

In the pond in the park
all things are doubled:
Long buildings hang and
wriggle gently. Chimneys
are bent legs bouncing
on clouds below. A flag
wags like a fishhook
down there in the sky.

The arched stone bridge
is an eye, with underlid
in the water. In its lens
dip crinkled heads with hats
that don't fall off. Dogs go by,
barking on their backs.
A baby, taken to feed the
ducks, dangles upside-down,
a pink balloon for a buoy.

Treetops deploy a haze of
cherry bloom for roots,
where birds coast belly-up
in the glass bowl of a hill;
from its bottom a bunch
of peanut-munching children
is suspended by their
sneakers, waveringly.

A swan, with twin necks
forming the figure three,
steers between two dimpled
towers doubled. Fondly
hissing, she kisses herself,
and all the scene is troubled:
water-windows splinter,
tree-limbs tangle, the bridge
folds like a fan.

May Swenson

53

Magic

A web
captures the storm:
glass beads, safe in fine net,
gather sunlight as they sway in
high winds.

Judith Nicholls

Shadows

Pictures
painted
by
the
sun

rubbed
out
by
the
clouds

*Gary
Boswell*

Sunset at Widemouth Bay

Fire
behind the sea –
the sky is full of long-winged angels
burning.

Wendy Cope

Ten Syllables for Spring

daffylonglegs
blowing
buttered trumpets.

Sue Cowling

The Oak and the Moon

Late one April afternoon I saw the moon
Caught in the outmost reach of an oak
Held fast in her cradle of wood
Biding her time
For the wind to shake her free.

Catherine Benson

Full Moon
II

When
the glim
skyweed slides
over the starfish sea,
and the foggy boulders slope
over the blue black ocean
over your head,
and the honing wind cuts corners,
slapping the flags in a gaunt light,
flogging the branches,
over and over,
and the heart trembles
in its heavy little house,
and you slip out,
and you look up
at that witchwax lamp in the dark,
crossing the gloved palm of heaven,
bright
as five pee in a figgy pudding,
and you wish
you wish you could
sleep.

William Bealby-Wright

Autumn

A touch of cold in the Autumn night –
I walked abroad,
And saw the ruddy moon lean over a hedge
Like a red-faced farmer.
I did not stop to speak, but nodded,
And round about were the wistful stars
With white faces like town children.

T. E. Hulme

November Night

Listen . .
With faint dry sound,
Like steps of passing ghosts,
The leaves, frost-crisped, break from the trees
And fall.

Adelaide Crapsey

Winter morning

Frost
sharpens
church spires
to a fine point,
pares down trees
to their
deep-set
bones.

Moira Andrew

Animals out of the cage

Swansong

Swan, swim over the sea.
    Swim, swan, swim!
Swan swim back again.
    Well swum, swan.

Trad.

Grey Goose and Gander

Grey goose and gander
Waft your wings together
And carry the good King's daughter
Over the one-strand river.

Anon.

Woolly Mammoth

He grazed sweet upland pasture,
crushing spring flowers
with hairy elephant feet,
methodically eating.
But sweeter plants grew
at the torrent fringe;
his long tusks clunked the stones,
trying the edge,

too far.

His roar shook snow
to plunge with him
into the crevasse where he lay,
ice-cradled, for centuries.

Discovered by explorers
after fifty thousand years
he was still wrapped in chestnut hair;
the broken tusks
were fossil ivory.
In his mouth were remnants of
that last surprising meal;
buttercups and orchids.

Irene Rawnsley

Hodmandod Riddle

Though not a cow
I have horns;
Though not an ass
I carry a pack-saddle;
And wherever I go
I leave silver behind me.

Trad.

The Woodlice

I turned over the mossy brick with my toe,
There, in the hollow of the brick,
    lay a family of woodlice,
Cowering from the light.
I poked them with a twig,
One fell on its back,
And squirmed,
Its many legs fluttering,
I looked at its white rubbery underside,
    with its many legs.
I shivered and wriggled,
All the woodlice in England seemed
    to crawl over me.
The grey wrinkled backs and bodies
    pressed into the brick,
Trying to escape from the light.
I was in the shadows,
But to the woodlice,
It was a furnace of hell.

Edmund Broadbent

from Paradise Lost (Book 7)

Forthwith the sounds and seas, each creek and bay
With fry innumerable swarm, and shoals
Of fish that with their fins and shining scales
Glide under the green wave, in schools that oft
Bank the mid sea: part, single or with mate,
Graze the sea weed their pasture, and through groves
Of coral stray, or sporting with quick glance
Show to the sun their waved coats dropped
                                    with gold,
Or in their pearly shells at ease, attend
Moist nutriment, or under rocks their food
In jointed armour watch: on smooth the seal,
And bended dolphins play: part huge of bulk
Wallowing unwieldy, enormous in their gait
Tempest the ocean: there Leviathan
Hugest of living creatures, on the deep
Stretched like a promontory sleeps or swims,
And seems a moving land, and at his gills
Draws in, and at his trunk spouts out a sea.

John Milton

Sunday Morning

The dizzying mill-wheel rests; the anvil's din
Hath ceased; all, all around is quietness.
Less fearful on this day, the limping hare
Stops, and looks back, and stops, and looks on man,
Her deadliest foe. The toil-worn horse, set free,
Unheedful of the pasture, roams at large;
And, as his stiff unwieldy bulk he rolls,
His iron-armed hoofs gleam in the morning ray.

James Grahame

Mallard

Squawking they rise from reeds into the sun,
climbing like furies, running on blood and bone,
with wings like garden shears clipping the misty air,
four mallard, hard winged, with necks like rods
fly in perfect formation over the marsh.

Keeping their distance, gyring, not letting slip the air,
but leaping into it straight like hounds or divers,
they stretch out into the wind and sound their horns
                                                    again.

Suddenly siding to a bank of air unbidden
by hand signal or morse message of command
downsky they plane, sliding like corks on a current,
designed so deftly that all air is advantage,

till, with few flaps, orderly as they left earth,
alighting among curlew they pad on mud.

Rex Warner

An Arrant Gull!

This is some creature of the elements
Most like your sea-gull. He can wheel and whistle
His screaming song, e'en when the storm is loudest –
Take for his sheeted couch the restless foam
Of the wild wave-crest – slumber in the calm,
And dally with the storm. Yet 'tis a gull,
An arrant gull, with all this.

Sir Walter Scott

Wonder

Collie puppies in a dooryard,
Wheeling along lopsided,
So hard to manage those hind legs,
Standing, blue eyes on nothing,
Noses twitching,
Stubby tails in the air,
Trying to remember what they are thinking about:

Fat puppies that forget everything,
Even the terrible
White teeth their mother yaps at them
When she eats her supper:

Fat puppies full of wonder
At round holes where spiders live,
At the wide wings of a yellow butterfly,
And lifting shrill voices of wonder
At the stranger who leans over their gate
Making uncouth noises.

Bernard Raymund

71

Skeletons of Mice

We found them in the quarry there:
Small, perfectly formed, bleached white by the sun;
lying all neatly arranged where death
had reached out and touched them;
each bone where it should be
and all joined together, just like those you see
in pictures in encyclopædias.

Thinking about them, we wondered what
had happened – did a cat
catch them among the rocks with quick claws
and, not being hungry, leave them there to bleed?
Then I remembered that
I had a pet mouse once that died because
I forgot to feed it.

We stood and gazed at them, talking in whispers:
small, white, perfectly white small bones,
that once had been skittering brown life.

Then I dug a hole with my knife,
and we put them in Richard's matchbox,
and we buried them under a strong red stone.
and we made them a cross out of two lolly sticks.
and then we went home.

Tony Charles

Riddle

I am a small iridescent twig,
Silver wrapped like a thin sweet.
A catch-sun, though you will not catch me,
Too quick as I skim the waters I came from.
When I pause on a reed or a lily's landing pad
I'm watching you as you marvel.
You look again: I've gone!

John Cotton

Dragonfly

Birds

early on the lawn
an immaculate hunter;
robin, dressed to kill

a celebrity,
this high-trapezing seagull
autographs the sky

sober roosting gulls
in this exotic sunset
become flamingoes

Irene Rawnsley

74

Woodlouse

Armoured dinosaur,
blundering through jungle grass by
dandelion-light.

Knight's headpiece, steel-hinged
orange-segment, ball-bearing,
armadillo-drop.

Pale peppercorn, pearled
eyeball; sentence without end,
my rolling full-stop.

Judith Nicholls

The Snake Song

Neither legs nor arms have I
But I crawl on my belly
And I have
Venom, venom, venom!

Neither horns nor hoofs have I
But I spit with my tongue
And I have
Venom, venom, venom!

Neither bows nor guns have I
But I flash fast with my tongue
And I have
Venom, venom, venom!

Neither radar nor missiles have I
But I stare with my eyes
And I have
Venom, venom, venom!

I master every movement
For I jump, run and swim
And I spit
Venom, venom, venom!

John Mbiti

Leopard

Gentle hunter
His tail plays on the ground
While he crushes the skull.

Beautiful death
Who puts on a spotted robe
When he goes to his victim.

Playful killer
Whose loving embrace
Splits the antelope's heart.

Yoruba

The Mighty Horse

Hast thou given the horse strength?
Hast thou clothed his neck with thunder?
Canst thou make him afraid as a grasshopper?
The glory of his nostrils is terrible.
He paweth in the valley, and rejoiceth in
                                        his strength:
He goeth on to meet the armed men.
He mocketh at fear, and is not affrighted;
Neither turneth he back from the sword.
The quiver rattleth against him,
The glittering spear and the shield.
He swalloweth the ground with fierceness and rage:
Neither believeth he that it is the sound of the
                                        trumpet.
He saith among the trumpets, Ha, ha;
And he smelleth the battle afar off,
The thunder of the captains, and the shouting.

Book of Job

Buffalo Dusk

The buffaloes are gone.
And those who saw the buffaloes are gone.
Those who saw the buffaloes by thousands and how
    they pawed the prairie sod into dust with their
    hoofs, their great heads down pawing on in a
    great pageant of dusk,
Those who saw the buffaloes are gone.
And the buffaloes are gone.

Carl Sandburg

Fishbones Dreaming

Fishbones lay in the smelly bin.
He was a head, a backbone and a tail.
Soon the cats would be in for him.

He didn't like to be this way.
He shut his eyes and dreamed back.

Back to when he was fat, and hot on a plate.
Beside green beans, with lemon juice
squeezed on him. And a man
with a knife and fork raised, about to eat him.

He didn't like to be this way.
He shut his eyes and dreamed back.

Back to when he was frozen in the freezer.
With lamb cutlets and minced beef and prawns.
Three months he was in there.

He didn't like to be this way.
He shut his eyes and dreamed back.

Back to when he was squirming in a net,
with thousands of other fish, on the deck
of a boat. And the rain falling
wasn't wet enough to breathe in.

He didn't like to be this way.
He shut his eyes and dreamed back.

Back to when he was darting through the sea,
past crabs and jellyfish, and others
like himself. Or surfacing to jump for flies
and feel the sun on his face.

He liked to be this way.
He dreamed hard to try and stay there.

Matthew Sweeney

Objects made from words

Mower

Horned beast
Savage mouth
Tungsten steel teeth
Shirring shearing
Sneering across the lawn
Flower heads flying.

Sweet smell of cut grass
Green spray over a prow
And a wash of trim topped leaves.
An inner wake, a wave of guilt,
Memories of petalled foam,
Of flower heads flying.

Catherine Benson

Dustbin Liner

The ghost of all our rubbish come to haunt us.
A ragged crow that blows about the garden.
A giant's burnt rice pudding skin.
Black ice waiting to be skidded on.
The shroud of many unimportant things.
A limbless, bulging belly.
A cauldron brewing garbage soup.
A witch's plastic mac.
The envelope for a long black letter.
The silent hungry beggar at my door.

Sue Cowling

Simultaneously

Simultaneously, five thousand miles apart,
two telephone poles, shaking and roaring
and hissing gas, rose from their emplacements
straight up, leveled off and headed
for each other's land, alerted radar
and ground defense, passed each other
in midair, escorted by worried planes,
and plunged into each other's place,
steaming and silent and standing straight,
sprouting leaves.

David Ignatow

'I like to see it lap the miles'

I like to see it lap the miles,
And lick the valleys up,
And stop to feed itself at tanks;
And then, prodigious, step

Around a pile of mountains,
And, supercilious, peer
In shanties by the sides of roads;
And then a quarry pare

To fit its sides
And crawl between
Complaining all the while
In horrid, hooting stanza;
Then chase itself down hill

And neigh like Boanerges;
Then, prompter than a star,
Stop – docile and omnipotent –
At its own stable door.

Emily Dickinson

from **Antony and Cleopatra**

The barge she sat in, like a burnished throne,
Burnt on the water: the poop was beaten gold;
Purple the sails, and so perfumed that
The winds were love-sick with them. The oars
                                    were silver,
Which to the tune of flutes kept stroke, and made
The water which they beat to follow faster,
As amorous of their strokes.

William Shakespeare

87

from The Duchess of Malfi

Princes' images on their tombs
Do not lie, as they were wont, seeming to pray
Up to heaven; but with their hands under
                        their cheeks
(As if they died of the toothache) – they are
                        not carved
With their eyes fixed upon the stars; but as
Their minds were wholly bent upon the world,
The selfsame way they seem to turn their faces.

John Webster

Inside My Zulu Hut

It is a hive
without any bees
to build the walls
with golden bricks of honey.
A cave cluttered
with a millstone,
calabashes of sour milk
claypots of foaming beer
sleeping grass mats
wooden head rests
tanned goat skins
tied with *riempies**
to wattle rafters
blackened by the smoke
of kneaded cow dung
burning under
the three-legged pot
on the earthen floor
to cook my porridge.

Mbuyiseni Oswald Mtshali

*riempies – thongs (Afrikaans)

A Riddle

I am an instrument, a pipe,
A bright brass concertina
Making heavenly music.
Planets, spheres, the Plough, the Milky Way
All come at my calling
Winking at me, eye to eye,
As if they knew that he who plays me well
Will understand them, entering
The mystery of the universe and bringing closer
Infinite secrets held for aeons
In the darkness which I penetrate.

Play me in silence, and I'll give you
Silence in return
Though in your head, professor,
You'll be seeing stars.

John Mole

Telescope

Two Totleigh Riddles

I am a see-through pear
Hanging from my treeless branch.
A bit of a conjuror I can ripen suddenly,
Or disappear at a switch.
Like the apple I am good for you
Lengthening your days.

My momentary delights
Are held close
In a paper bud.
I flower best at night,
My petals falling
Like bright showers
When I am fired to beauty.

John Cotton

Firework

Light Bulb

Riddle a Thousand Years Old

I wrestle with the waves and war with the wind;
Firmly I fight against their combined forces,
When down beneath them I dive to discover
                                    the earth.
My native land is to me unknown.
Standing still I am strongest in the struggle;
If I move, their might is more than mine,
And soon they destroy me and sap my strength,
Meaning to carry away what I keep in guard.
I foil them if my bones break not,
If the rocks hold steady against my strength.
Now, if you know me, name my name.

from **The Exeter Book**

An Anchor

92

Riddle Written on an Ancient Manuscript

I saw four strange creatures travelling together;
They left behind them a trail of black tracks.
The lifter of birds sailed up speedily,
It took to the air, then dived under the waves.
The struggling warrior who points out the paths
To the four creatures, crawled on and on
Over the rich gold. What was it I saw?

from **The Exeter Book**

Two Fingers, a Thumb and a Quill Pen

93

Three Riddled Riddles

1. I have nine legs
   I carry an umbrella.
   I live in a box
   at the bottom of a ship.
   At night
   I play the trombone.

   What am I?

   Answer: I've forgotten.

2. You see me at dawn
   with the clouds in my hair.
   I run like a horse
   and sing like a nightingale.
   I collect stamps
   and coconuts.

   What am I?

   Answer: I'm not sure.

3. I taste like grapefruit.
   I swim like a chair.
   I hang on the trees
   and people tap my face,
   rake my soil
   and tell me jokes.

   What am I?

   Answer: I've really no idea.

Martyn Wiley & Ian McMillan

Why Are Fire Engines Red?

Two and two is four
Three times four is twelve
Twelve inches is a ruler
Queen Mary was a ruler
Queen Mary ruled the sea
There are fish in the sea
The fish have fins
The Finns fought the Russians
The Russians are Red
Fire engines are always rushin'
That's why fire engines are red.

Anon.

Hear my voice

What For!

One more word, said my dad,
And I'll give you what for.

What for? I said.

That's right, he said, what for!

No, I said, I mean what for?
What will you give me what for for?

Never you mind, he said. Wait and see.

But what is what for for? I said.

What's what for for? he said,
It's to teach you what's what,
That's what.

What's that? I said.

Right, he said, you're for it,
I'm going to let you have it.

Have what? I said.

Have what? he said,
What for, that's what.
Do you want me to really give you
Something to think about?

I don't know, I said,
I'm thinking about it.

Then he clipped me over the ear.

It was the first time he'd made sense
All day.

Noel Petty

Quarrel

He says to me, he says,
D'you want a thick ear? he says.
Who? I says.
You! he says.
Me? I says.
Yes, he says.

I says, Oooh.

Trad.

The Juggler's Wife

Last night, in front of thousands of people,
he placed a pencil on his nose
and balanced a chair upright on it
while he spun a dozen plates behind his back.
Then he slowly stood on his head to read a book
at the same time as he transferred the lot
to the big toe of his left foot.
They said it was impossible.

This morning, in our own kitchen,
I ask him to help with the washing-up —
so he gets up, knocks over a chair,
trips over the cat, swears, drops the tray
and smashes the whole blooming lot!
You wouldn't think it was possible.

Cicely Herbert

Aaaaaagh!

Aaaaagh! I screamed
for no
reason
at all.

Martin Doyle

The Little Girl

The scratchy couch at my grandmother's
creaked as she pointed to a little girl
in a class photograph.
'And who's this?'
I brought the album
close to my face to decide.
All my brain would tell me was
'It's you, of course,
don't you even know yourself
when you see yourself?'
'It's me' I said,
although I couldn't remember
any of the girls or the dress.
'Look again' she said.

Julie O'Callaghan

To P.J. (2 Yrs Old Who Sed Write a Poem for Me in Portland, Oregon)

if i cud ever write a
poem as beautiful as u
little 2/yr/old/brotha,
i wud laugh, jump, leap
up and touch the stars
cuz u be the poem i try for
each time i pick up a pen and paper.
u. and Morani and Mungu
be our blue/blk/stars that
will shine on our lives and
make us finally BE.
if i cud ever write a poem as beautiful
as u, little 2/yr/old/brotha,
poetry wud go out of bizness.

Sonia Sanchez

105

Getting back home

Hang your hat on the peg
Rest up, rest up
Fling your coat on the bed
For you have travelled many miles to see me.

Put your feet on the bench
Rest up, rest up
Heave off your heavy boots
For you have come through Winter days to see me.

Settle down by the fire
Rest up, rest up
Lean back and smile at me
For after all this time and travelling
Oh traveller, I'm glad to see you.

Jenny Joseph

Micky Thumps

As I was going down Treak Street
For half a pound of treacle,
Who should I meet but my old friend Micky
                                    Thumps?
He said to me, 'Wilt thou come to our party?'
   I thought a bit,
   I thought a bit,
   I said I didn't mind:
   So I went.

As I was sitting on our doorstep
Who should come by but my old friend Micky
                              Thumps's brother?
He said to me, 'Wilt thou come to our house?
Micky's ill.'
    I thought a bit,
    I thought a bit,
    I said I didn't mind:
    So I went.

And he were ill.
He were gradely ill.
He said to me,
'Wilt thou come to my funeral man, if I die?'
    I thought a bit,
    I thought a bit,
    I said I didn't mind:
    So I went.

And it were a funeral!
Some stamped on his grave:
Some spat on his grave:
But I scraped my eyes out for my old friend
                              Micky Thumps.

Anon.

108

The Donkey's Owner

Snaffled my donkey, he did – good luck to him! –
Rode him astride, feet dangling, near scraping
                            the ground.
Gave me the laugh of my life when I first see them,
Remembering yesterday – you know, how
                         Pilate come
Bouncing the same road, only that horse of his
Big as a bloody house and the armour shining
And half Rome trotting behind. Tight-mouthed
                         he was,
Looking he owned the world.
                      Then to-day,
Him and my little donkey! Ha! – laugh? –
I thought I'd kill myself when he first started.
So did the rest of them. Gave him a cheer
Like he was Caesar himself, only more hearty:
Tore off some palm-twigs and followed shouting,
Whacking the donkey's behind . . . Then suddenly
We see his face.
The smile had gone, and somehow the way he sat
Was different – like he was much older – you know –
Didn't want to laugh no more.

Clive Sansom

A Sunnit to the Big Ox

(Composed while standing within two feet of him,
and a tuchin' of him now and then.)

All hale! thou mighty annimil – all hale!
You are 4 thousand pounds, and am purty wel
Perporshund, thou tremendjus boveen nuggit!
I wonder how big yu was when yu
Was little, and if yure mother would no yu now
That yu've grone so long, and thick and fat;
Or if yure father would rekognise his ofspring
And his kaff, thou elephanteen quadrupid!
I wonder if it hurts yu much to be so big,
And if yu grode it in a month or so.
I spose wen yu was young tha didn't gin
Yu skim milk but all the creme yu could stuff
Into yore little stummick, jest to see
How big yu'd gro; and afterward tha no doubt
Fed yu on oats and hay and sich like,
With perhaps an occasional punkin or squosh!
In all probability yu don't know yure anny
Bigger than a small kaff; for if yu did
Yude break down fences and switch yure tail,
And rush around and hook and beller,
And run over fowkes, thou orful beast.
O, what a lot of mince pies yude maik,
And sassengers, and your tail,
Whitch can't weigh fur from forty pounds,
Wud maik nigh unto a barrel of ox-tail soup,
And cudn't a heep of staiks be cut off you,
Whitch, with salt and pepper and termater
Ketchup, wouldn't be bad to taik.
Thou grate and glorious inseckt!

But I must close, O most prodijus reptile!
And for mi admiration of yu, when yu di,
I'le rite a node unto yure peddy and remanes,
Pernouncin yu the largest of yure race;
And as I don't expec to have half a dollar
Again to spair for to pay to look at yu, and as
I ain't a dead head, I will sa, farewell.

Anon.

111

The Greengrocer's Love Song

Do you carrot all for me?
My heart beets for you.
With your turnip nose
And your radish face
You are a peach.
If we canteloupe
Lettuce marry.
Weed make a swell pear.

Anon.

The Snoddywig

Maa-a-a?
Yes, my dear.
Maaaaa-a-a?
Yes, my dear.
Maa-aa, do plums have legs?
No, my dear.
Then danged if I ain't ate a snoddywig!

Trad.

Sarky devil

Our teacher's all right, really,
But he can't stop making
These sarcastic remarks.

Nev Stephens, who's got no one to get him up,
Creeps in fifteen minutes late
Practically every morning –
Always with a new excuse.
And old Sarky says,
'Good evening, Stephens,
And what little piece of fiction
Have you got for us today?'

He even sarks the clever kids:
Says things like
'Proper little Brain of Britain, aren't we?'
And only yesterday when Maureen
(Who's brilliant at everything)
Complained of a headache,
He says, 'Perhaps it's the halo
Pinching a bit, Maureen.'

And then there's Bill Nelson
Who's just one of these naturally scruffy kids
Who can't keep anything clean –
Well, his homework book's a disgrace,
And Sarky holds it up
Delicately, by a corner,
At arm's length, and he says,
'Well, Lord Horatio,
Did you have your breakfast off this
Before or *after* the dog had a chew at it?'

Even the one who's getting sarked
Laughs –
Can't do much else, really;
And the rest of the class
Roars, of course,
And feels like one big creep.

It's a good job we understand
Old Sarky.

Eric Finney

Zimmer's Head Thudding Against the Blackboard

At the blackboard I had missed
Five number problems in a row,
And was about to foul a sixth,
When the old, exasperated nun
Began to pound my head against
My six mistakes. When I cried,
She threw me back into my seat,
Where I hid my head and swore
That very day I'd be a poet,
And curse her yellow teeth with this.

Paul Zimmer

Advertisement

Are your children peaky and thin?
Too many late nights? Too much telly?
Forest air and a fattening diet
  Will very soon put things right!

A week or two at Sweetmeat Cottage
Is bound to make them scrumptiously chubby.
Children just love my gingerbread house,
  My liquorice doors and chimneys.

There's everything here to delight a child,
And one kind lady to see to their needs —
For I love children, tasty little darlings!
  Apply without delay.

C. J. D. Doyle

Memories

This afternoon I sifted through
those old and stained brown photos.
You and the others looked so good,
but I looked pathetic
dressed in my p.e. kit.

Martin Doyle

117

He Wishes for the Cloths of Heaven

Had I the heavens' embroidered cloths,
Enwrought with golden and silver light,
The blue and the dim and the dark cloths
Of night and light and the half-light,
I would spread the cloths under your feet:
But I, being poor, have only my dreams;
I have spread my dreams under your feet;
Tread softly because you tread on my dreams.

W. B. Yeats

Amaze

I know
Not these my hands
And yet I think there was
A woman like me once had hands
Like these.

Adelaide Crapsey

The Shoes

These are the shoes
Dad walked about in
When we did jobs
In the garden,
When his shed
Was full of shavings,
When he tried
To put the fence up,
When my old bike
Needed mending,
When the car
Could not get started,
When he got up late
On Sunday.
These are the shoes
Dad walked about in
And I've kept them
In my room.

These are not the shoes
That Dad walked out in
When we didn't know
Where he was going,
When I tried to lift
His suitcase,
When he said goodbye
And kissed me,
When he left his door-key
On the table,
When he promised Mum
He'd send a postcard,
When I couldn't hear

His special footsteps.
These are not the shoes
That Dad walked out in
But he'll need them
When he comes back home.

John Mole

The Mother's Song

It is so still in the house,
There is a calm in the house;
The snowstorm wails out there,
And the dogs are rolled up with snouts
                                under the tail.
My little boy is sleeping on the ledge,
On his back he lies, breathing through
                                his open mouth.
His little stomach is bulging round –
Is it strange if I start to cry with joy?

Eskimo

from The Task

I would not have a slave to till my ground,
To carry me, to fan me while I sleep,
And tremble when I wake, for all the wealth
That sinews bought and sold have ever earned.
No: dear as freedom is, and in my heart's
Just estimation prized above all price,
I had much rather be myself the slave,
And wear the bonds, than fasten them on him.

William Cowper

Cautions

He that spendeth much,
   And getteth nought;
He that oweth much,
   And hath nought;
He that looketh in his purse
   And findeth nought—
He may be sorry,
   And say nought.

He that sweareth
   Till no man trust him;
He that lieth,
   Till no man believe him;
He that borroweth
   Till no man lend him,—
Let him go where
   No man knoweth him.

Hugh Rhodes

Poems to see and hear

There It Is Right Under Your Nose ←

I lost a poem the other day.   ↑
I only put it down for a minute,   Bit further.
And when I turned round   ↑
It was gone.   No further up.

I searched the house
From top to bottom.   ↑
I hunted high and low.
I even looked   Up there.
In the back of my mind
And on the tip of my tongue
But it was nowhere to be found. ↑

Wait a minute.   →   →   There it is.

John Coldwell

125

The Alphabet Speaks Up!

A   YOU
B   QUIET
C   HERE
D   LIGHTED TO MEET YOU
E   BY GUM
F   YOU LIKE
G   UP
H   OCOLATE
I   SPY
J   MES IS MY FRIEND
K   TE IS MY FRIEND TOO
L   NOT TELL YOU AGAIN
M   TALKING TO YOU
N   AND OUT
O   DEAR
P   NUTS
Q   HERE
R   YOU READY?
S   IT RAINING?
T   TIME
U   SMELL
V   RY NICE
W   DOUBLE ME
X   MARKS THE SPOT
Y   STOP NOW?
Z   WHO?

SAID ME!

David Horner

One Old Oxford Ox

One old Oxford ox opening oysters;
Two teetotums totally tired trying to
                              trot to Tadbury;
Three tall tigers tippling tuppeny tea;
Four fine foxes fanning fainting friars;
Five flighty flibbertigibbets foolishly fishing for flies;
Six sportsmen shooting snipes;
Seven Severn salmons swallowing shrimps;
Eight Englishmen eagerly examining Europe;
Nine nimble noblemen nibbling noodles;
Ten tinkers tinkling upon ten tin tinder-boxes
                              with ten tenpenny tacks;
Eleven elephants elegantly equipt;
Twelve talkative tailors trimming tartan trousers.

Trad.

127

A Counting Poem

wan
do
tree
fear
fife
seeks
siphon
eat
neighing
den
elephan'
twirl

Bob Cobbing

Simple Seasons

Swallows,
Primroses
Return.
It's
New,
Green!

Skylarks
Up,
Meadows
Motley,
Elms
Regal.

Apples
Untold,
Trees
Unruly;
Mists
Now.

Waters
Icebound,
Naked
Trees;
Earth
Rests.

Eric Finney

rock sand tide

Dom Silvester Houédard

Ah Choo!

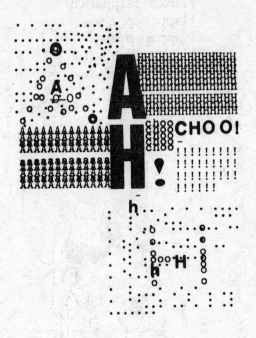

Liam O'Gallacher

Fury of Sneezing

Tesch,   Haisch, Tschiiaa
           Haisch, Tschiiaa
           Haisch, Happaisch
           Happapeppaisch
           Happapeppaisch
           Happapeppaisch
           Happapeppaisch
           Happa peppe

                   TSCHAA!

Kurt Schwitters

132

The Loch Ness Monster's Song

Sssnnnwhuf ff fll?
Hnwhuffl hhnnwfl hnfl hfl?
Gdroblboblhobngbl gbl gl g g g g glbgl.
Drublhaflablhaflubhafgabhaflhafl fl fl—
gm grawwwww grf grawf awfgm graw gm.
Hovoplodok-doplodovok-plovodokot-
                              doplodokosh?
Splgraw fok fok splgrafhatchgabrlgabrl fok splfok!
Zgra kra gka fok!
Grof grawff gahf?
Gombl mbl bl—
blm plm,
blm plm,
blm plm,
blp.

Edwin Morgan

Q

Q
Kew
Queue
Cue
Q

Coo!

Bob Cobbing

Snake Riddle

Why didn't the viper
Vipe 'er nose?
Because the adder
'ad 'er 'andkerchief.

Anon.

Horrible Riddle

How did the intruder get in?
In t'rough der window.

Anon.

Character studies

The Fishmonger

Sleek through his fingers
the fishes slide,
glisten and curve
and slap their tails
on the smooth white slab . . .

silver on marble
ranged they lie.

The fishmonger's hands
are cold with eternal
halibut, haddock,
hake and cod;

his arms are swollen
and red beside
the delicate silver
of the slender fishes;

but his eyes are glazed
and dull like theirs
and his mouth gapes
in codlike wonder

at the flickering stream
that slips through his fingers!

A. S. J. Tessimond

Ouch!

Theophilus Thrapplethorn,
  The celebrated thistle-sifter,
While sifting a sieve of unsifted thistles,
  Thrust three thousand thistles
Through the thick of his thumb.
  If Theophilus Thrapplethorn
The successful thistle-sifter,
  Thrust three thousand thistles
Through the thick of his thumb,
  See that thou,
When thou siftest a sieve of thistles,
  Dost not get the unsifted thistles
Stuck in thy thumb!

Anon.

It was stuffy in the classroom.
He put his hand inside his desk,
feeling for a pencil. It was cool
in there, he let his hand swing aimlessly around.
The space within seemed vast, and when
he reached in further he found
nothing, could feel no books, no ruler.
His hand floated as if in a bath of shadows,
airy and refreshing, not at all
the same place that the rest of him was in.

He put both arms in, let them drift
deeper, this way and that. It was more than empty.
The inside had no sides. His hands

never reappeared through some unexpected hole.
He lifted the lid quietly a little more. A waft
of soft air cooled his face, the same
as on summer nights or under leafy trees.

He bent his head down to the gap. He looked inside.
Dark as deep water, deep as a clear night sky.
He smiled. He put his head inside.
'What are you doing?' asked the teacher. But he
                                                didn't hear.
He slid his shoulders in, and then,
before anyone could reach to stop him,
he bent from the waist, kicking his chair back,
and with a muffled cry of pleasure
dived. For a split second
as the room filled with fresh air,
we watched his legs slide smoothly down
                                        into the desk
and disappear. And then the lid fell back, shut with a
                                        soft thud.

Dave Calder

Written in a Happy Mood

The old man is nearly seventy.
He behaves like a little boy.
He shouts with joy when he sees berries growing,
He chuckles with delight at the antics of acrobats.

While the rest are gathering stones to build a
                                    summer house
He stands alone, staring at his reflection in the pond;
Tucked under his arm is a dog-eared book,
Like the first time he went off to school.

Lu Yu

from Beowulf

Now from the marshlands under the mist-mountains
Came Grendel prowling; branded with God's ire.
This murderous monster was minded to entrap
Some hapless human in that high hall.
On he came under the clouds, until clearly
He could see the great golden feasting place,
Glimmering wine-hall of men. Not his first
Raid was this on the homeplace of Hrothgar.
Never before though and never afterward
Did he encounter hardier defenders of a hall.

Anon. (Anglo-Saxon)

The Ghoul

When nights are dark and ways are foul,
Beware the fierce, ferocious ghoul
Who'd tear the heart from out your breast
To make his kind of scrumptious feast.
He'll pull a rider off his horse
To eat them both and then, what's worse,
He'll swallow down a poor man's ass,
He won't let any traveller pass.
He eats the small, he eats the great,
All living flesh to him is meat,
Indeed the ghoul's a fearful threat
And clever. If you think he's *there*,
You'll find he's really *over here*.
One person found a tree to climb,
The ghoul just tore him limb from limb,
With really quite amazing ease,
And ended all his mortal lease.
The ghoul, I think, is rather gross,
I would not count his death a loss,
If someone did him in, brave soul,
No one would mourn this horrid ghoul.

John Sweetman

from The Grave

Oft in the lone churchyard at night I've seen,
By glimpse of moonshine chequering through
                             the trees,
The schoolboy with his satchel in his hand,
Whistling aloud to keep his courage up,
And lightly tripping o'er the long flat stones
(With nettles skirted and with moss o'ergrown),
That tell in homely phrase who lie below.
Sudden he starts, and hears, or thinks he hears,
The sound of something purring at his heels;
Full fast he flies, and dares not look behind him,
Till out of breath he overtakes his fellows;
Who gather round and wonder at the tale
Of horrid apparition, tall and ghastly,
That walks at dead of night, or takes his stand
O'er some new-opened grave, and (strange to tell!)
Evanishes at crowing of the cock.

Robert Blair

'in Just -'

in Just -
spring   when the world is mud-
luscious the little
lame balloonman

whistles   far   and wee

and eddieandbill come
running from marbles and
piracies and it's
spring

when the world is puddle-wonderful

the queer
old balloonman whistles
far   and   wee
and bettyandisbel come dancing

from hop-scotch and jump-rope and

it's
spring
and
    the

        goat-footed

balloonMan   whistles
far
and
wee

e. e. cummings

People Who Must

I painted on the roof of a skyscraper.
I painted a long while and called it a day's work.
The people on a corner swarmed and the traffic cop's
    whistle never let up all afternoon.
They were the same as bugs, many bugs
                                on their way—
Those people on the go or at a standstill;
And the traffic cop a spot of blue, a splinter of brass,
Where the black tides ran around him
And he kept the street. I painted a long while
And called it a day's work.

Carl Sandburg

Seeing Granny

Toothless, she kisses
with fleshly lips
rounded, like mouth
of a bottle, all wet.

She bruises your face
almost, with two
loving tree-root hands.

She makes you sit, fixed.
She then stuffs you
with boiled pudding and lemonade.

She watches you feed
on her food. She milks
you dry of answers
about the goat she gave you.

James Berry

147

Lost in France

He had the plowman's strength
In the grasp of his hand.
He could see a crow
Three miles away,
And the trout beneath the stone.
He could hear the green oats growing,
And the sou'-west making rain;
And the wheel upon the hill
When it left the level road.
He could make a gate, and dig a pit,
And plow as straight as stone can fall.
And he is dead.

Ernest Rhys

The Fat Lady's Request

I, too, will disappear, will
Escape into centuries of darkness.

Come here and give me a cuddle,
Sit on my lap and give me a hug

While we are both still enjoying
This mysterious whirling planet.

And if you find me fat, you find me
Also, easy to find, very easy to find.

Joyce la Verne

A Vampire Considers Buying a New Mirror

On
Reflection
No.

Peter Mortimer

The Ever-touring Englishmen

The ever-touring Englishmen have built their
                                    bungalows
All over our sweet forest
They drive their trains with smoke
O look at them, how they talk on wires to one
                                    another
With their wires they have bound the whole world
                    together for themselves.

Gond

My People

The night is beautiful,
So the faces of my people.

The stars are beautiful,
So the eyes of my people.

Beautiful, also, is the sun.
Beautiful, also, are the souls of my people.

Langston Hughes

Pass the Parcel

One unwraps it carefully
One rips
One is slow
One drops it
One shakes
One stares
One is missed
One listens
When the music stops
the packet is between
One wins
One cries
Music starts again

Phil Rampton

Mirror

The baby in the pushchair
is like an old man on a bus.
He wears a wool hat
and a cardigan.
He smiles at the view
and talks to himself,
but at home, in the night,
sometimes,
he cries.

The old man on the bus
is like a baby in a pushchair.
He wears a wool hat
and a cardigan.
He smiles at the view
and talks to himself,
but at home, in the night,
sometimes,
he cries.

Martyn Wiley & Ian McMillan

Rules of Conduct

Do all the good you can,
By all the means you can,
In all the ways you can,
In all the places you can,
At all the times you can,
To all the people you can,
As long as ever you can.

John Wesley

The Great Panjandrum

So she went into the garden
to cut a cabbage-leaf
to make an apple-pie;
and at the same time
a great she-bear, coming down the street,
pops its head into the shop.
What! no soap?
            So he died,
and she very imprudently married the Barber:
and there were present
the Picninnies,
        and the Joblillies,
            and the Garyulies,
and the great Panjandrum himself,
with the little round button at top;
and they all fell to playing the game of catch-as-
                        catch-can,
till the gunpowder ran out at the heels of their boots.

Samuel Foote

154

INDEX OF FIRST LINES

155

ACKNOWLEDGEMENTS

The editor and publishers gratefully acknowledge permission to reproduce copyright poems in this book:

'Winter morning' by Moira Andrew, by permission of the author; 'Full Moon I' and 'Full Moon II' by William Bealby-Wright, by permission of the author; 'Mower' and 'The Oak and the Moon' by Catherine Benson, by permission of the author; extract from 'Beowulf' translated by Gerard Benson, reprinted by arrangement with Poems on the Underground; 'Seeing Granny' by James Berry from When I Dance, copyright © James Berry, 1988 reprinted by permission of Hamish Hamilton Children's Books; 'Shadows' by Gary Boswell from It's Brilliant, copyright © Gary Boswell, 1987 reprinted by permission of Stride; 'Seven Activities for a Young Child' by Alan Brownjohn from Collected Poems, reprinted by permission of the author and Century Hutchinson Ltd; 'desk' by Dave Calder, by permission of the author; 'Skeletons of Mice' by Tony Charles, by permission of the author; 'ab . . . yz . . . ic . . . qed', 'Q' and 'A Counting Poem' by Bob Cobbing, reprinted by permission of the author; 'There It Is Right Under Your Nose' by John Coldwell, by permission of the author; 'Sunset at Widemouth Bay' by Wendy Cope, by permission of the author; 'Riddle' and 'Two Totleigh Riddles' by John Cotton, by permission of the author; 'Dustbin Liner' and 'Ten Syllables for Spring' by Sue Cowling, by permission of the author; 'in Just -' is reprinted from Tulips and Chimneys by e. e. cummings, edited by George James Firmage, by permission of Liveright Publishing Corporation: copyright © 1923, 1925 and renewed 1951, 1953 by e. e. cummings: copyright © 1973, 1976 by the Trustees for the e. e. cummings Trust: copyright © 1973, 1976 by George James Firmage, and by permission of Grafton Books; 'Freedom' by Mary Dawson, by permission of the author; 'Advertisement' by C. J. D. Doyle, by permission of the author; 'Aaaaaagh!' and 'Memories' by Martin Doyle, reprinted from My P.E. Kit and Other Problems by Martin Doyle (Spine Journals, 1986) by permission of the author; 'Sarky devil', 'Simple Seasons' and 'Haiku', 'Hicuckoo!', 'Highcoo' by Eric Finney, reprinted by permission of the author; 'Coochi-coochi' by Bill Greenwell, by permission of the author; 'The Juggler's Wife' by Cicely Herbert, reprinted by permission of the author; 'The Alphabet Speaks Up!' by David Horner, by permission of the author; 'rock sand tide' by Dom Silvester Houédard, reprinted by permission of the author; 'My People' by Langston Hughes, copyright © 1926 by Alfred A. Knopf, Inc. and renewed 1954 by Langston Hughes, reprinted from Selected Poems of Langston Hughes, by permission of the publisher; 'Simultaneously' by David Ignatow, copyright © 1964 by David Ignatow, reprinted from Figures of the Human by permission of Wesleyan University Press; 'Their Beauty Has More Meaning' by Robinson Jeffers, copyright © Robinson Jeffers, 1947, reprinted from Selected Poems by Robinson Jeffers, by permission of Random House, Inc.; 'Getting back home' by Jenny Joseph, by permission of the author; 'The Fat Lady's Request' by Joyce la Verne, by permission of the author; 'The Snake Song' by the Revd Professor John Mbiti, reprinted by permission of the author; 'A Riddle', 'The Shoes' and 'Working in Winter' by John Mole, by permission of the author; 'The Loch Ness Monster's Song' by Edwin Morgan, reprinted from Poems of Thirty Years by Edwin Morgan, published by Carcanet Press Ltd by permission of author and publisher; 'A Vampire Considers Buying a New Mirror' by Peter Mortimer, reprinted by permission of the author; 'Inside My Zulu Hut' by Mbuyiseni Oswald Mtshali, copyright © Mbuyiseni Oswald Mtshali 1971, reprinted from *Sounds of a Cowhide Drum* (1971) by permission of Oxford University Press; 'Woodlouse' by Judith Nicholls, reprinted by permission of Faber and Faber Ltd from *Midnight Forest* by Judith Nicholls, and 'Magic' by Judith Nicholls, by permission of the author; 'The Little Girl' by Julie O'Callaghan, reprinted from *Edible Anecdotes* by Julie O'Callaghan (Dolmen Press 1983), by permission of the author; 'What For!' by Noel Petty, by permission of the author; 'Spell of Creation' by Kathleen Raine, reprinted by permission of the author; 'Pass the Parcel' by Phil Rampton, by permission of the author; 'Birds' and 'Woolly Mammoth' by Irene Rawnsley, by permission of the author; 'Child on Top of a Greenhouse' by Theodore Roethke, copyright © 1946 by Editorial Publications, Inc. from *The Collected Poems of Theodore Roethke* reprinted by permission of Doubleday, a division of Bantam, Doubleday, Dell Publishing Group, Inc. and Faber and Faber Ltd; 'To P.J. (2 Yrs Old Who Sed Write a Poem for Me in Portland, Oregon)' by Sonia Sanchez, reprinted by permission of Broadside Press, Detroit; 'Buffalo Dusk' and 'People Who Must' from *Smoke and Steel* by Carl Sandburg, copyright © 1920 by Harcourt Brace Jovanovich, Inc. and renewed 1948 by Carl Sandburg, reprinted by permission of the publisher; 'The Donkey's Owner' by Clive Sansom, reprinted from *Collected Poems* by Clive Sansom, published by Methuen by permission of David Higham Associates Ltd; 'Fury of Sneezing' by Kurt Schwitters, reprinted from *PIN* (Gaberbocchus Press) by permission of Jasia Reichardt and Edith Thomas; 'Forsythia' by Mary Ellen Solt, reprinted from *Flowers in Concrete* by Mary Ellen Solt, published by Indiana University Fine Arts Department (1966) by permission of the author; 'Fishbones Dreaming' by Matthew Sweeney, reprinted by permission of the author and Usborne Publishing Ltd; 'Jack and Jill' and 'The Ghoul' by John Sweetman, by permission of the author; 'Water Picture' by May Swenson is reprinted by permission of the author, copyright © 1956, May Swenson, and first appeared in *The New Yorker Magazine*; 'The Fishmonger' by A. S. J. Tessimond, reprinted by permission of Hubert Nicholson; 'I Am a Prose Poem' by Nick Toczek, reprinted by permission of the author; 'Mallard' by Rex Warner, reprinted from *Poems* by Rex Warner, by permission of the estate of Rex Warner and The Bodley Head Ltd; 'Three Riddled Riddles' and 'Mirror' by Martyn Wiley and Ian McMillan, by permission of the authors; 'Zimmer's Head Thudding Against the Blackboard' reprinted from *The Republic of Many Voices* by Paul Zimmer (October House, Inc. 1969) by permission of the author.

Every effort has been made to trace copyright holders, but in a few cases this has proved impossible. The editor and publishers apologize for these cases of unwilling copyright transgression and would like to hear from any copyright holders not acknowledged.